How To be Fr
by Joe Blow

Cover image from http://www.123rf.com/

Joe Blow, *How to Be Free*© 2012, Joe Blow

ALL RIGHTS RESERVED. This book contains material protected under International and Federal Copyright Laws and Treaties. Any unauthorized reprint or use of this material is prohibited. No part of this book may be reproduced or transmitted in any form or by any means, electronic or mechanical, including photocopying, recording, or by any information storage and retrieval system without express written permission from the author / publisher.

The Author

Joe Blow is the pseudonym for a man who, though currently happy and high functioning, has had a long history of mental illness, including endogenous depression, bipolar disorder and obsessive compulsive disorder. This book is the product of a lifelong struggle to integrate flashes of insight and powerful symbols which appeared to him, often during what we might define as psychotic episodes, with observable reality and a rudimentary knowledge of science by appropriating useful concepts from the work of such iconoclastic thinkers as Wilhelm Reich, R. D. Laing, Keith Johnstone, William Blake and Oscar Wilde.

If asked whether this approach and this conceptual framework have provided him with a secure foundation for emotional stability, happiness and flowering creativity, Blow would reply, "Well, so far so good."

Contents

Introduction...4
What I'm Not...10
Why Joe Blow?...11
The Love of Perfection is the Root of All Evil...12
What is God?...13
Radical Self-Acceptance...15
Armouring...17
What Is the History of the Human Neurosis?...19
Our Individual Experience...28
My Own Journey...32
Sexuality...36
Sexual Fixations...42
What is the Imagination?...44
The Scary Side of the Imagination...45
Degrees of Being Alive...47
Depression...50
Self-Acceptance in a Troubled World...53
Emotional Scars...57
Compassion is Projected Self-Pity...58
The Inner Child...60
What is Consciousness?...62
Impasses to Thought...69
Fight Against Only that Which You Wish to Become...72
Violence is Admission of Error...75
A New World is Rising...77
General Advice on Becoming Free...80
Keith Johnstone...82
A Closing Message...83
Feedback...84

Introduction

The aim of this book is to set you free. But free from what? Free from neurosis. Free from the feeling that you have to obey authority. Free from emotional intimidation. Free from addiction. Free from inhibition.

The key to happiness, mental health and being the most that we can be is absolute and unconditional self-acceptance. The paradox is that many of our problems are caused by trying to improve ourselves, censor our thinking, make up for past misdeeds and struggling with our negative feelings whether of depression or aggression.

But if we consider ourselves in our entirety in this very moment, we know these things :

1. Anything we have done is in the past and cannot be changed, thus it is pointless to do anything else but accept it. No regrets or guilt.

2. While our actions can harm others, our thoughts and emotions, in and of themselves, never can. So we should accept them and allow them to be and go where they will. While emotions sometimes drive actions, those who completely accept their emotions and allow themselves to feel them fully, have more choice over how they act in the light of them.

Self-criticism never made anyone a better person. Anyone who does a "good deed" under pressure from their conscience or to gain the approval of others takes out the frustration involved in some other way. The basis for loving behaviour towards others is the ability to love ourselves. And loving ourselves unconditionally, means loving ourselves exactly as we are at this moment.

This might seem to be complacency, but in fact the natural activity of the individual is healthy growth, and what holds us back from it is fighting with those things we can't change and the free thought and emotional experience which is the very substance of that growth.

Divide and conquer - that is a key philosophy in military

campaigns. And the same applies to the individual. An individual at war with themselves is easily dominated or controlled by others. If we want to become a free individual the way to do so is through individuation, allowing the divided parts of our nature to integrate into a unified whole.

We may feel that there is within us a battle between the desire to do things we feel are right and the desire to do things we feel are wrong. The battle of good and evil.

But what are good and evil?

Good is that which contributes to the health of the individual or the society or wider ecological system of which they are a part.

So what do we mean by evil? We could say that evil is anything which adversely effects the health of the individual or the system. But the term "evil" is a very strong one. Selfishness has a negative impact on the health of the system by interfering with the free flow of material, information or energy. But we wouldn't consider minor acts of selfishness, like eating more than our share of a piece of cake, to be evil. Evil is a term we use to describe those acts which cause significant suffering or otherwise do major harm. The essence of evil is the imposition of the will. If we take something from somebody against their will - their life, their property, their dignity, their humanity - this is clearly evil. But also it is an act of evil to try to control another's behaviour through fear or guilt or other forms of deliberate manipulation. The fact that such behaviour has a dire impact on the health of the individual and the social system can be demonstrated when we consider that the worst forms of socially-sanctioned cruelty we know of - the Holocaust, the witch burnings, the Spanish Inquisition, the stoning to death of women by the Taliban - have been the work of societies in which the repression and control of the individual through fear and/or guilt were the norm.

Of course there is such a thing as necessary evil. We have to impose our will on those who behave destructively towards others, etc. But it must be recognised that this does not solve the problem of evil. At best it contains it. But, more often than not, even this is an illusion and the act of using our will to contain evil sows the seeds of more evil behaviour. Only the healing of individuals and of society can actually decrease the incidence of evil.

But what we need to understand, if we are to understand ourselves, is our own impulses to engage in destructive or dominating behaviour towards others.

If we have such impulses they originate in a lack of acceptance of some aspect of ourselves. Hostility towards others or the need to control others is projected self-contempt.

It is commonly acknowledged that the hostility of some heterosexual men towards gay men is due to a lack of acceptance of their own denied homosexual impulses. The same applies to all forms of hostility. Those who wish to hunt animals for sport, or otherwise mistreat them, don't want to accept that they are animals themselves and thus physically vulnerable in the same ways. Those who wish to harm children feel threatened by their disowned inner child. Men who wish to harm women are threatened by their disowned feminine side.

Anyone who is fully accepting of themselves feels no hostility toward others. They may be troubled by the hostility of others and oppose it, but they will not experience feelings of hostility themselves. If a wild animal attacks us, we may be distressed and do what we can to protect ourselves, even to the extent of killing the animal, but, if we are sensible, we feel no hostility towards that animal, recognising that it is behaving according to its nature. Our feelings about the hostility of other humans would be the same if we did not have in ourselves something of what they express in their hostile behaviour. Those who scream for the death penalty after a vicious crime, if not loved ones of the victim, are those who know that they have within them the same kind of rage as the criminal and feel the need for a harsh penalty for such crimes in order to feel secure in their ability to control themselves.

From this we can see that evil behaviour originates in our neurosis (our divided state) and is not an expression of our primary nature.

We also need to look at the phenomenon of selfishness.

Historically we've criticised ourselves for being selfish. Sin is the religious term for selfishness and religions sometimes teach that selfishness should be a source of shame.

By contrast, some modern thinkers view selfishness as the essential nature of living things. They feel that the imperative for the survival and propagation of the genes is the driving force behind the behaviour of all animals, including humans.

Both of these ways of looking at the human phenomenon of selfishness are mistakes.

We humans are different from other animals in that we have the ability to connect with each other and the world around us through the use of our intellect and imagination. This brings into our emotional life priorities and drives of which other animals know nothing. Our egos are unchained from the necessities of brute survival, and the emotional rewards that guide our behaviour come not just from making babies, but also from finding out why apples fall out of trees or painting the ceiling of the Sistine Chapel. Many individuals express the meaning of their lives in emotionally satisfying ways but choose not to propagate their genes. As entities capable of higher reasoning we have a choice. Other animals generally do not.

So if the source of human selfishness is not a genetic imperative, what is it?

Quite simply it is the symptom of a system which is sick and, as a result, in pain. This is perfectly natural. Try hitting your thumb with a hammer, and then try to turn your attention to something other than the pain. It is very difficult. When a living system such as the human organism is sick or in pain the natural thing is for it to turn its attention towards itself. I know from my own experience that when I was suffering from depression it was very hard for me to pay attention to anyone else's situation or feelings. But when I am happy I forget myself much of the time and concentrate on the interesting phenomena of other people - their lives, their thoughts and their feelings.

It is important to emphasise that this healthy state of outward-directedness is not the same as selflessness. Selflessness if taken literally is a meaningless term. If we had no self we would not exist, since the term "self" is our expression for the totality of which we consist. But we use the term selfless as an opposite to selfish, i.e. to describe a state of mind in which the needs of others take precedence over our own needs. Such a state of mind can occur during an emergency when an individual will risk their life to save someone else. Or it can be a state of mind consciously cultivated through an effort to repress or transcend selfish impulses. But this is the problem with the concept when it comes to trying to understand the nature of the healthy psyche. We can understand the pathological nature of selfishness, but to assume that selflessness is the epitome of the psychological health of the individual carries the danger that we may feel that being healthy means repressing our personal needs or desires in favour of those of others. This would just be swapping one form of sickness for another.

Our selfishness is not wrong. It is appropriate when we are sick and suffering to concentrate on addressing our need for relief from this state. The only problem is that we don't know how to best help ourselves. We are able to give comfort to ourselves through distraction and materialism, and this is what we should do in the absence of a cure. This is the equivalent of taking aspirin when we have a fever. It won't cure the problem, but it will make us feel better in the mean time.

The aim here is to clarify the nature of the illness and identify practical approaches to treatment which address the root cause.

Any form of submission, including submission to any kind of ideal, is unhealthy. The healthy individual is one who does only what they wish to do. This is O.K. as the desire to do anything destructive is non-existent in the healthy individual.

The way to eliminate the desire to do anything destructive is through radical self-acceptance. And this is also the cure for selfishness. The pain of neurosis is that of the individual at war with his or her thoughts and feelings. The path to healing is to learn to accept our thoughts and feelings unconditionally.

We live in a society in which hostility and selfishness are the norm. We live in a profoundly neurotic society.

Now to say that our society is a neurotic one and that neurosis is the norm may seem ludicrous or even offensive. But there is a simple test you can use to discover whether or not you are neurotic.

Is your mind more like a playground or more like a prison? If it is more like a prison then you are neurotic.

But don't worry. This book is a "Get Out of Jail Free" card and a passport back into the playground.

What I Am Not

Let me explain here that I have never done any academic training in the field of psychology. I'm not an expert, at least in that sense.

I'm an individual who has suffered greatly from depression throughout a significant portion of my life. And I've been diagnosed as being bipolar, having experienced several psychotic breakdowns.

The thinking which has lead to the ideas I express here has been driven by two things -

1. A desire to work out why human society functions so poorly and can lead to such terrible phenomena as the World Wars and the Holocaust. In my adolescence I began asking myself why, if at base what we most want is to be loved, then why don't we all just love each other. Are killing our enemies and accumulating wealth not poor substitutes for the kind of happiness we could have if we did that?

2. A desperate need to find a way out of a tangled state of despair so great that I twice tried to take my own life.

I offer these thoughts for what they may be worth. I trust that, if there is anything of truth in them, it will prosper, and if there is anything which is a mistake it will be seen as such and rightly dismissed.

All I can say is that these are the thoughts which, for me, have stood the test of time. For the last few years, as these ideas have become more clear in my head and I've overcome my reluctance to believe in myself, I've been free of depression and my creative abilities have flowered.

Why Joe Blow?

Joe Blow is a name used for someone who is nobody special. This is an appropriate pseudonym for me to use because it emphasises that I take no credit for any useful ideas or insights that might be contained in this work.

Nobody creates ideas or truths. They simply exist. We either see them or we don't. And the fact that we may see them is not a sign of strength or achievement on our part. It takes an act of will to maintain a delusion, to cling to a belief in spite of any contrary evidence. But when we have useful ideas or discover truths it is often because we lack the will or the ability to protect ourselves against them.

I've never had a very effective ego, hence my history of depression and psychosis. I'm not a brave individual. I wouldn't have gone to those frightening places if I had known how not to.

I'm only moderately intelligent. And also only moderately well-read.

I haven't put much effort into any of this, beyond the effort we all put into keeping ourselves afloat emotionally.

So, to the extent that these ideas may be useful, it is a quality of the ideas themselves alone, and has nothing to do with the individual who gives expression to them. No doubt at this very moment many other individuals are expressing similar ideas, as any of us might if we learn to relax and be simply who we are and not who we think we should be.

The Love of Perfection is the Root of All Evil

Most of us accept that it would be unreasonable to expect ourselves to be perfect, but we still see perfection as an ideal, something to be pursued. And yet to pursue perfection, if such a thing even exists, makes about as much sense as pursuing death.

If anything were ever perfect it would be sterile. It would be a dead end.

Everything wonderful in the whole universe has grown out of imperfection. That is how the creative principle of the universe works.

The universe is a system - a network of energy, some of which behaves in a particular kind of orderly way that we refer to as matter. This matter exists in a web of action and interaction with other matter and forms of energy. And some of that matter is alive and operating under its own internal direction as a subsystem of the whole. And the most complex form of that living matter is ourselves as we look out into the universe and try to understand it.

But how did we come about? Through a serious of mutations, i.e. imperfections. Perfection is a steady-state. But the creative principle operates through variation. An animal, for instance, is born which is not quite right, a mutation of some kind. If that variation, that imperfection, proves beneficial then something new and wonderful comes into existence, a new branch on the tree of life. And all of those imperfections led to us.

And yet we somehow became intolerant of our mistakes and imperfections instead of seeing them as an intrinsic part of the creative process of the universe.

How this unhelpful way of thinking about ourselves took hold is a mystery we can speculate about a bit later. To get an idea of what an insidious hold it has had upon us historically we need to examine the idea of God.

What is God?

We often have a tendency to personify the impersonal. We talk of Mother Nature or Father Time. Of course there is no actual Mother Nature, but the earth's ecosystem on which we may put this human face, does exist.

This is the case with the concept of God. There is no God, anymore than there is a Mother Nature, but the creative principle of the universal system is an observable reality. There are laws to the way the universe operates that allow for orderly phenomena and for the evolution of more basic forms into more complex and capable forms such as ourselves. And onto this reality, for our own comfort, we put a human face.

This may sound very cold. But we should remember that all the wonders of our world and the rest of the universe and ourselves are a product of the operation of these laws.

And when we realise that these laws operate within human society in the form of love then we can see that the identification of this mythical figure with a healing or comforting social phenomena is not inappropriate.

But what of the concept of an angry God who asks us to subjugate ourselves to him. This is where the concept of the love of perfection as the root of all evil can best be understood.

By the time the Judaeo-Christian concept of God (differing greatly from those deities of earlier times which often represented only certain aspects of nature or the human psyche) came into being, our society was profoundly neurotic. Civilisation (i.e. repression) had been going on for a long time. A neurotic society is generally controlled by its most neurotic members as long as they are still capable of functioning, because their insecurity makes the control of those less neurotic than themselves an imperative. When we are neurotic, we live in fear of the disowned part of our own nature, and, if unchecked, this fear can manifest itself as the desire to control those who express it or represent it in the external world.

For reasons which will be explained later, the human neurosis first appeared in males. It quickly spread to women, but, in general, men tended to be more neurotic. And thus, as we and our society became more neurotic, men felt the need to take control and impose their will to an ever greater degree. Our societies, which in the distant past had been matriarchal because of the primacy of the reproductive role, became patriarchal. This is why God was conceived as not only a man, but an angry, neurotic, intolerant man. Because of the phenomenon known as projection, we create our Gods in our own image, just as we see in the world around us a projection of ourselves.

Paranoia is an important symptom of neurosis. We have a tendency to project the disowned part of ourselves, which we fear, onto others. For example, during the Cold War, capitalists saw in communism a projection of their own conscience which told them that it was wrong to be greedy, and communists saw in capitalists a projection of their own unacknowledged awareness of the futility of trying to repress their greed through discipline.

In a practical sense, fear of God was a way of maintaining the neurotic order of society. One might feel that a sick, miserable, evil society was better than no society at all, a collapse into unstructured barbarism. After all some kind of structure was needed if we were to co-operate enough to develop science and learn to understand ourselves and our world better.

But the major problem was that the root of the sickness was lack of self-acceptance, and by holding God up as an ideal of perfection and preaching that humans needed to abase themselves before "him", the churches were making the sickness much much worse.

The view of God expressed depends on the individual. Since Jesus was clearly relatively free of neurosis, his concept of a loving, forgiving and tolerant God was more in keeping with an accurate understanding of the functioning of a healthy system.

Radical Self-Acceptance

Let's take a look at what self-acceptance means in practice.

I'll use an example from my own life. When I was around 20 I went through a terrible depression. A new mother was staying in our house with her baby. At a point early in the depression an image occurred to me of myself throwing the baby down onto the floor and killing it. In my imagination those present didn't worry about the baby but turned their attention to me and asked what made me do such a thing. At first I dismissed this thought, but it just wouldn't go away and over time it came to obsess me, and I thought that I might actually carry it out. After the mother and baby left, when this was no longer a possibility, I continued to spiral deeper and deeper into depression. "How could I even think about such a terrible thing?" I asked myself. "Surely I must be evil. There must be some horrible sickness in me." And the more I tried to find a solution to this problem the worse it got.

Since then I've learned more about what we call Obsessive Compulsive Disorder and discovered that this kind of thinking and the accompanying anxiety and depression are incredibly common.

If I had simply accepted that this was something that my mind had thrown up, and that, since it was a thought and not an action, it was morally neutral, the problem would not have occurred. By "trying to be a good person" and struggling with this thought, I only made myself miserable, and, as a result, for the time I was depressed, a more selfish person, and thus someone who took more from those around him than he gave. So accepting these thoughts would have not just been doing the right thing by myself, but also by others.

We have limited control over what we think or feel. We do have some control. We can distract ourselves or learn disciplines such as meditation. But often this is not a good idea.

The natural tendency in the mind is to seek wholeness. We can make ourselves miserable quite easily by clinging to ideas by an act of will or trying to fight against the ideas and feelings which come to us unbidden.

Armouring

So what form does this human neurosis take?

The psychiatrist Wilhelm Reich wrote about a phenomenon he called "armouring". According to him there are two forms of armouring - body armour and character armour. The purpose of armouring is protection from what is inside and what is outside.

Body armour involves the storing of repressed emotions in the musculature of the body. A good example is the archetypal stiff upper lip. Reich found that, by observing the body, one could see the undealt with emotions, and massage of certain parts of the body could bring on a cathartic release of anger, tears, feelings of grief, etc. and free the body up to experience more pleasurable experiences such as sexual arousal.

Character armour is a fixed ego structure - an inflexible, defensive way of thinking about ourselves and similarly inflexible, defensive way of behaving. The behaviour of the armoured individual could be described as stereotyped or habit-bound. This is the opposite of the open, spontaneous approach to life which was our original nature.

Reich described this armour as : "a protection of the ego against external and internal dangers. As a protective mechanism which has become chronic it can rightly be called armour... in unpleasurable situations the armouring increases, in pleasurable situations it decreases. The degree of character mobility, the ability to open up to a situation or to close up against it constitutes the difference between the healthy and the neurotic character structure." *The Function of the Orgasm* (translated by T.P. Wolfe, Panther, 1968)

On the larger scale it is possible to relate this to forms of thinking exhibited by groups of individuals. In some groups we find the free expression and exchange of ideas, while others are bound up in unquestioned dogma. Such dogma, which we may find in religious groups or political organisations for example, is another form of armouring aimed at protecting the group against criticism from the outside and the insecurity of free thought and doubt within.

What Is the History of the Human Neurosis?

I'm not a biologist or palaeontologist. This is just a loose theoretical framework which I've put together from pieces of other theories and my own imagination.

The process of evolution has expressed itself in a multitude of living creatures, each taking advantage of the potential of its own niche in the ecosystem. The natural system of which any animal or plant is a part places limitations on its behaviour. For instance a population which breeds too much might find itself exceeding the carrying capacity of its immediate environment and having to migrate or die off.

But within these limits, the vitality of the species resides in the fact that each individual tries to maximise its mating opportunities. This is how species become stronger. Since those who are healthiest can win the competition to mate, the stronger genes are propagated more often than the weaker ones.

This process is very effective, but it carries with it a serious weakness. It limits the capacity for co-operation and thus achievement through group effort. These forms do occur in non-human animals quite extensively, for instance in the case of a pride of lions co-operating to hunt an antelope, but the full potential for co-operative achievement is always compromised by competition for mating. Hive insects have a co-operative society which seems to have minimal internal competition, but they also appear to be an evolutionary dead-end, although, unlike the dinosaurs, an environmentally sustainable one.

Humans breached this impasse.

In any animal species in which the infant bonds with the mother for any length of time after birth, the nature of the new-born infant is to be unconditionally loving. Love is simply open spontaneous communication and learning is absorption of information by observation. The infant, being a blank slate in terms of discriminatory thinking, will bond with the mother without discriminating in any way. This is what makes that bonding possible, and explains why some animals will bond with a human and act as if they were the mother. But, in most species, the period of this bond is short because the need to fight for survival in a harsh environment takes over. The individual's behaviour is determined by an interplay of instincts, which are a part of the physical operating structure of the animal and common to all members of that species, and learned behaviour, either directly competitive or co-operative when needed to meet short term ends such as pack hunting to provide a collective meal.

A capacity for imagination and intelligence is inherent in complex brains. Just as life is an experimental process in which more complex living systems can form over time and survive or not depending on fitness for interacting with, making use of and living within the limits of the environment, so thinking works the same way within the individual brain and the society of which it is a part. Imagination and insight are functions of open spontaneous unstructured information sharing within the brain. This is the opposite of stereotypical thinking, i.e. thinking which follows strict pathways. The brain function of most animals is dominated by stereotypical thinking because, most of the time, this is what works most effectively in meeting the challenges of the struggle for survival and the mating imperative. While there might be times when a little lateral thinking would be beneficial, stopping to think would generally be a liability to survival, so that potential in the brains of those species did not develop.

The longer the nurturing period the more of a chance the species has of developing a co-operative social culture and with it higher intelligence. The mother's instinct to nurture may be driven by the imperative to protect and foster her own genes, but it shelters the infant's original unconditionally loving nature, with its capacity for freely imaginative thought, and allows it to flourish rather than be subsumed by the survival imperative. Intelligence and imagination were potentials just waiting for the right environment in which to develop.

Our ape-like ancestors lived in the fertile Rift Valley of

Africa, where there was plenty of food and relatively few predators, thus allowing the females to nurture their offspring for a longer time. (The nurturing period of humans is longer than that of any other animal.) This liberated our intellect and allowed us to form a co-operative, non-competitive society. Freed from the battle for survival, we began to look at the world around us and wonder how it worked and what it meant.

Some other species developed close co-operative social bonds and, with them, at least the rudiments of intelligence. One can see these qualities in the behaviour of some of the ape species and also sea mammals such as whales and dolphins. One major advantage that we humans have however is hands with opposable thumbs. The apes are not as intelligent as us, but even if they were, they would not have been able to develop technology with their clumsy hands and thus they couldn't make full use of that intelligence. And whales and dolphins are stuck in the sea and have no hands with which to manipulate their environment.

So if our origins were idyllic, what went wrong?

There was a problem. While predators were less prevalent they were not nonexistent. The group was vulnerable to animals such as leopards which might find us easy pickings.

The women had to concentrate on rearing the young, so the job of protecting the group from leopards fell to the men.

We are learning machines and thus we adapt to our environment and the nature of the tasks we undertake. Within the tribal home openness and love and spontaneity were the order of the day. But once we went out to kill the leopards which threatened us we had to adapt to a different kind of environment - a hostile one - and a different kind of task - one which required discipline and hostile behaviour from ourselves. If we were to effectively protect the tribe from leopards we had to become like leopards.

Now if this behaviour had been limited to the hunt, everything might have been fine. But it is hard to entirely successfully divide oneself into two separate mindsets, one for home and one for work. The men would have been bound to bring some of the aggressiveness and competitiveness they learned on the hunt back into the previously harmonious tribal home.

All of us were new to this. Our understanding was limited, and what mattered was maintaining the stability of the group. The women were worried that this aggressive behaviour would compromise the harmony of the tribal home and thus have a detrimental influence on the infants. And so they criticised the behaviour of the men. In this harmonious society, criticism of one individual by another had rarely been necessary.

At first this would not have been a big problem, we were still very healthy and thus very flexible. What made it a big problem is that there was no solution. Gradually, over time, it would increase. The more the men felt criticised at home the more time they would want to spend on the hunt. And they went from hunting only predators, to hunting animals for food. Previously we had been vegetarians.

There was one powerful approach to this problem, but it was not, in itself, a solution, and that was sex.

Sex is clearly necessary for reproduction. It fulfills that function in all mammals. But, in more social mammals, it fulfills a second function, that of social bonding. We can see this particularly in the behaviour of very social mammals such as the bonobos and dolphins.

One way to bond with another individual or ease the tension of any form of emotional conflict, is through the mutual exchange of pleasurable sensation. While reproduction requires sexual contact between the male and the female, the use of erotic pleasure for social ends need not be restricted to male/female activity. And thus we find that, among bonobos, dolphins and other species, sexual activity occurs also between members of the same sex.

The bonobos, our nearest genetic relatives, spend a lot of time rubbing genitals. Adult males generally won't rub genitals with their mothers, but otherwise these genital exchanges are not restricted by age or gender or kinship. Bonobos do not form permanent relationships. And bonobo society is matriarchal. Male bonobos are bigger and stronger, but the females are more closely bonded with each other and thus the centre of power.

This gives us some clue as to what the life of the earliest humans might have been like - matriarchal, no pair bonding to compromise the communal whole and sexual behaviour bisexual and largely indiscriminate, acting as a kind of social glue through shared pleasure.

It is important to point out here that this was pre-neurosis, pre-armouring, and therefore sexuality would not have taken any of the armoured forms that it did later. Armoured sex can be a conduit for anger and, in the extreme, can morph into rape.

The natural response of the women of the tribe to the increasingly rowdy behaviour of the men would have been to try to socialise them through sex. This was already something which was used to foster the bonding of the group, so when there was a threat to that bonding it would be natural to increase that behaviour and focus it on those members who were threatening the stability of the whole.

No doubt the men were also using sex to bond amongst themselves. But sex between the men and the women would have taken on a profound significance at this time.

We have to remember that the basic nature of the men was to be unconditionally loving. This was their nature at birth and was fostered by the nurturing process and the harmony of their society. To the extent that they had had to learn to suppress that nature and copy the behaviour of the leopards, they were no longer whole. They had laid a conflicting program over their original one and this would have compromised their sense of emotional security. While hunting provided an outlet for the frustration of living a divided existence, at base they longed for their new persona to be reconciled with their original nature.

Thus sex came to fulfill a third role. First it was about reproduction. Then it was about social bonding. In the third stage of its evolution it became about emotional healing through a physical union with an individual who represents the disowned part of our own nature. This is how the sexuality of most males became fixated on women and the sexuality of most women became fixated on males. Bisexuality was our first nature, this was our second nature, and soon I will consider the development of exclusive same sex fixations.

But sex, while very helpful in slowing down the process of men's developing neurosis, couldn't halt it.

It was around this time that we developed our conscience. The conscience is the code of the society internalised as a part of the individual's ego. So, at first, we would allow our behaviour to be guided by the criticisms of others. But, not wanting to be the subject of social approbation, at some stage we would start to second guess, we would internalise the rules and tell ourselves off for going against them before anyone else had the opportunity. The pain we felt when our behaviour conflicted with the rules of the conscience is what we call guilt.

The conscience, while it tended to cause us pain and thus make us more self-centred, did keep a lid on extreme expressions of hostility. Later in history there would be exceptions to this in which some individuals and societies developed consciences which saw some kinds of hostility as being in service of what they saw as the good. It was under these circumstances that most of the greatest human atrocities have been committed - witch burnings, The Spanish Inquisition, The Holocaust, "ethnic cleansing", genocide against tribal cultures and war. Here the concept that some group of people were evil, made it seem to the individual's conscience that any form of hostility heaped upon them was in the service of the good.

Because the rules of this society were principally those of the females who kept the home together, the men began to become more and more prone to feelings of guilt about their competitive hunting lifestyle. They weren't actually doing anything wrong (they were taking care of aspects of the needs of the group) but it felt wrong. And the more wrong they felt, the more insecure they became, and the more insecure they became the angrier they became and thus the more destructive they became, and then they really were doing things which they could see were doing harm to the group. And so on and so on. Stopping the process would have required either explaining to themselves and the women what was happening, which they didn't yet have the insight to do, or saying they were wrong which they knew was not the case. If they didn't defy the implication that they were in the wrong they would have collapsed into a state of inoperable self-contempt or depression. The more insecure and condemned they felt the more angry and egotistical and defiant they became, and armouring was the form that this took in the shape of their personalities. The initial substance with which we built our armour was repressed anger. This is why, when the armour is compromised, a release of anger or even violence is the result.

Over time, the whole of the group became insecure and armoured. Hostility within the group and the strain of desperately trying to use sex to socialise the men put a strain on the women and compromised the nurturing of the children. We all ended up getting hurt. And, in our pain, we turned within and began to build a wall that we thought would keep us safe.

As we males became more and more egotistical and more fragile in our sense of ourselves, drastic changes in social behaviour had to take place in order to hold the group together.

This was the origin of monogamy. The only way to keep men from fighting over the sexual favours of women was to institute strict controls on sexual behaviour.

Of course this meant that both men and women had to adopt sexual repression. We could no longer simply do what we wanted when it came to our sexual behaviour. But the desires were not gone. We still wanted to have sex with different people, but we had to push those desires down and contain them. In this way, repressed sexual desires became a part of the substance of our armouring in the same way that repressed aggressive feelings had become before this.

This is when fear of sex became a significant part of our psychology and our society. When we were not armoured, sex had been an unthreatening and pleasant part of our lives, and something which was beneficial to our society.

But the armoured personality and the armoured society are built on sexual repression. Erotic feelings are essentially anarchic and could bring the whole thing down. And, unrestrained sexual behaviour in an armoured society leads to social conflict. We keep it all together by not sleeping with each other's partners and not confronting people with sexual arousing material which might make it hard for them to maintain their self-discipline.

Because our tertiary sexual drive is to reunite with the disowned part of our own nature, we came to select sexual partners whose appearance reminded us of our original state. This is how we developed our concept of female beauty. What we tend to think of as classical beauty is childlike features such as wide eyes, full lips, a slim build, and, in our originally hairy days, this included a shortage of hair. And so this is how we lost our hair. This is called selection for neotony and it explains why we look more like a chimpanzee foetus than we do like a full-grown chimp.

So eventually we became relatively hairless.

Primitive tribal societies often run around mostly or completely nude, but, as we became more armoured and found ourselves carrying around a powder keg of repressed sexuality, the wearing of clothes became a priority for us. They made us feel less personally vulnerable, but also they covered up the flesh of others which was a potential stimulus for our anarchic erotic feelings. If you are hungry, and you are on a diet, it is easier if all that yummy food is covered up. It helps you maintain your discipline.

Now we can see the significance of our myth about Adam and Eve in the Garden of Eden. They were naked and lived an idyllic existence. Then a predator (a snake in the story) inspired them to seek knowledge of good and evil (in this case the destructive behaviour of predators, which seemed evil to them in their idyllic state), and, as a result, they developed a sense of shame about their nudity. And they were expelled from the Garden, which is what ultimately happened to us. We became alienated from the natural world and condemned to a life in the wilderness of our own neurosis.

Over time we would develop cities which were external expressions of our own armoured state in which we would shelter from the natural world of which we no longer felt a part. This had the advantage of allowing us to work together in larger networks on the problem of understanding the world and ourselves. On the downside it allowed forms of social alienation such as loneliness, crime and homelessness to flourish. The invention of the internet makes urban living no longer necessary for networking, but we have too large a population for most of us to live any other way. Psychologically this isn't a problem as the emotionally healthy individual can thrive in a somewhat artificial environment. The only problem is reorganising our lives in such a way that our cities are ecologically sustainable.

Our Individual Experience

Our own early experiences in many ways mirrored what happened to us historically as a species.

When we were born we were an unconditionally loving bundle of physical needs.

We've touched on the meaning of love, but let's look at the phenomenon in more detail so that we know what we mean by the unconditionally loving nature of the infant.

It is all too easy to get love mixed up with adoration or compassion. Love is really a kind of communication. It is any communication which comes through the ego rather than from the ego. Love is when we are really with another person rather than somewhere else in our head. Love is characterised by paying attention and being spontaneous. When we are open to love every interaction with others changes us. We are closed off to love when our behaviour is stereotypical, when rigid character traits and ways of expressing ourselves interfere with open, spontaneous communication. This happens when our ego is insecure, caught up in attempts at self-justification, and when we feel the need to repress our feelings, whether of anger, grief, sexuality or whatever, and are afraid to be spontaneous lest it release those scary feelings. When we are able to really be with someone and open up spontaneous communication with them it can be accompanied by the deep feelings of warmth that we associate with the concept of love. But it is important here to concentrate on process rather than experience if we are going to understand the phenomenon. The reason why we generally experience love only for friends, sexual partners or family members, is that these are the people we know well enough not to be afraid to drop our defences with them. Our soul (or original self or inner child) loves everybody unconditionally, but when our ego is insecure it is too scared to open up to that love, except with those who reassure it with their indications of acceptance. This also explains some of the experiences which are common in charismatic religious gatherings. Provide a context in which people feel accepted and united with others and the capacity for experiencing love can surface, giving usually chronically ego-bound individuals a sense of something that seems totally magical and otherworldly. They see it as proof of the existence of a supernatural God and a confirmation of the philosophy of that particular church, while others might realise that the same kind of experience could come if the armouring of their ego had been compromised by the consumption of LSD.

Let's imagine ourselves first entering the world. We are unconditionally loving and we have needs - to be fed, cleaned, cuddled, etc. We interact with those around us in an open and spontaneous way. At first this may mainly be communicating about our needs - crying when we are hungry, etc. As we learn to walk and talk our ways of communicating, as well as the things we want to communicate about, increase.

The only problem is that we soon learn that not everyone wants to communicate openly and spontaneously with us. Maybe other children do, and our parents when they have the time to relax and play with us, but much of the time we find that adults are not really with us. They don't listen, or if they do they don't respond in ways which make sense to us. The feeling for us is like that of a child who enters a playground but finds that most of the other children don't want to play with him.

One of the most important things to understand about the mind of a child is that children always think it is their fault. This makes sense. If you come into a world, of course you are going to assume that those who already live there know what's what. To say, "I'm sane and they are all crazy!", would seem pretty desperate. How were we to know that that was the case? And this is why so many traumas happen in childhood which can warp us for life. "It must be my fault my parents got divorced," we tell ourselves, or, "I must be to blame for Uncle Pete going to jail, because it was my genitals he was caught playing with." If all we were dealing with was the thing itself, the effects of most misfortunes and abuses would pass away much more quickly. What causes the really deep scars is self-blame and the ego insecurity and thus obsession with self-justification and questions of self-worth that it engenders. This is what is meant by "the sins of the fathers are visited upon the sons". Sin is just a judgemental religious word for neurosis - for the self-obsession of the insecure ego.

Of course, if our parents were able to explain to us that they were fucked-up and insecure, and that it was nobody's fault, least of all ours, things would have been much easier for us. If we had parents who were blind or deaf or physically crippled, we wouldn't have felt bad about the fact that we could see or hear or run. It is not a case of our needs not being met. We didn't need our open and spontaneous communication to be responded to in kind. We were resilient beings who could be happy with however the world worked. The only problem was the conclusion that something was wrong with us.

This feeling that something was wrong with us meant that more and more of our thinking was taken up by attempts to find a way to prove it wrong. Our ego became insecure. This is the time in our development when we would start to "act naughty". The more we doubt our own worth the more we feel compelled towards acts of defiance. We project our insecurities onto the outside world and then fight against them in that arena. Later in life we may try to prove our worth by scrawling graffiti on a public building, fighting in a war or climbing Mount Everest, but when we are still in diapers we have to be satisfied with stealing candy bars in the supermarket or pulling the cat's tail. It was at this stage that we became angry. Anger is the emotion with which the insecure ego tries to defend itself when challenged.

This is when our parents had to start teaching us right from wrong. They gave us the blue print for our conscience. At first we might try to obey the rules our parents set in order to avoid punishment, but eventually they would become incorporated into our thinking about our own self-worth. We would feel any failure to live up to these standards was evidence of our worthlessness. We learned to feel guilty.

Two factors in our upbringing contributed to how neurotic,

i.e. armoured, we ended up. First was how positive our early interactions with others were, that is how little sense of blame we took onto ourselves to make us feel insecure. And the other was how restrictive the value system was which formed our conscience. (Although this normally happens in childhood, some of us adopt an ideology or religion later in life, thus changing the nature of our conscience.) If our experiences are bad, leaving us angry and insecure, but our conscience is not too restrictive, we needn't repress those feelings entirely. We might go out to heavy metal rock concerts, take drugs and fuck around, and thus not entirely loose access to our capacity for love, but, if we were born into a fundamentalist religious society, for instance, we would have to repress our rebellious expressions within a very restrictive form of social discipline (not to mention that the strict moral code would be a constant source of criticism to our insecure ego, thus increasing its anger), so we would end up very alienated indeed from our capacity for unconditional love. We could still feel love within the security of our own kind, but that is all.

My Own Journey

Sometimes we have a somewhat faulty concept of the nature of childhood innocence. We may think that the innocent child has an angelic nature. This is not true.

At the age of ten I asked my mother if we could go to a Grand Prix because I hoped to have the opportunity of witnessing a racing car driver die in a car crash.

This isn't the sort of thing most of us associate with the healthy child, but at that time I was psychologically healthy.

I was motivated by curiosity. I felt no hostility towards race car drivers. But I knew that they sometimes died painful deaths in car crashes on the speedway and I was curious to see what someone dying in that way would look like.

As I've said elsewhere, our original nature when we are born is one of unconditional love, i.e. we are open to the world and non-judgemental of what we find there. However we have no morality. A moral system is something we learn from adults. And we have no compassion. Since compassion is nothing more than projected self-pity, we do not develop the ability to feel compassion until we become a neurotic adult.

As a child I was emotionally strong, resilient and not easily hurt. I was often bullied, but I don't think I blamed the bullies for being bullies any more than I would blame a bee for stinging me. I was non-judgementally accepting of others.

One day in primary school, when I must have been about 6 or 7, one of the bullies got me in the toilets, told me to lay down on the floor, pulled down my pants and stuck wet wads of toilet paper up my arse. He told me that, if I didn't come back and let him do it again the next day I would die. Since I hadn't found the experience particularly pleasant, I decided not to come to him the next day. "If I die, I die," I told myself.

This was a temporarily uncomfortable and scary experience, much like a trip to the doctor to have an inoculation, but, in itself, it was of little significance to me.

Now if the same thing had happened to me when I was a neurotic teenager, full of self-doubt because of all of the aggressive feelings I'd been repressing and desperately uncomfortable about my own body because of the extreme form of sexual repression I'd been practicing since shortly after the onset of puberty, the experience might have been an almost rape-like ordeal. I was much more fragile emotionally in adolescence and adulthood than I had ever been in childhood.

I think that what makes childhood a vulnerable time and a time when the seeds of adult neurosis are sown is that it is the time when we are learning the lessons we will try to apply as an adult. We are building a conceptual framework about ourselves and the world. If we learn a lesson which is unhelpful it can warp our adult life up until the point at which we may unlearn it and thus free ourselves from our neurosis.

I think the lesson I learned which made life painful for me as an adult was to turn inwards. I always held onto the concept of accepting others unconditionally, and I wanted to understand them, but I think it must have been made clear to me early on that simply asking a bully why he is a bully was not going to work. I'm not sure if I ever tried it. I think not.

But if there was conflict in the world and I wanted to understand it, I think I must have decided to keep my head down, keep my thoughts to myself and take a passive approach to that conflict outwardly. If I hadn't been bullied I might not have taken this approach. The bullying itself didn't inflict all that much pain, but the lesson I learned from it led to me adopting a strategy which would almost kill me. (Perhaps if an adult had been able to perceive what I was doing to myself and give me guidance about it this wouldn't have happened. But when I've sought help for my problems throughout my life I've found that those who've tried to help me have their own problems and are often pretty clueless. Those who helped me the most were those like my mother and my psychiatrist who provided me with space and acceptance in which I could help to formulate my own self-understanding.)

The big problem with the introverted approach to life is that one tends not to allow oneself an outward expression for frustration, in the form of competitive activities or angry outbursts or whatever. If we bottle up our feelings of frustration then we are liable to take them out on ourselves. In my case, toward the latter part of my teens I became severely depressed and developed an obsession that I might gouge my own eyes out.

This can't be explained simply by the inward directing of anger. I think another factor was sexual repression. Soon after puberty I became mysteriously ashamed about masturbation. This had nothing to do with anything any adult had said to me as my parents had a laid back, healthy attitude about such things. But I went for several months without masturbating during which I felt a heavy cloud of condemnation hanging over my head. Later, during my twenties, the comfort and sense of connection to my repressed healthy self which I got from masturbating to pictures of naked women, was one of the few things to make my life bearable. But, at the same time, I felt this erotic element as something powerfully anarchic which could shake up my repressed state in ways which were very anxiety-provoking.

I think the third, and perhaps biggest factor, in my neurosis was the fact that I held on so tightly to the concept of unconditional love. The problem with it is that, the only way to keep this non-judgemental attitude alive in the absence of the resilient, flexible, amoral and non-compassionate innocent state is to, emotionally, take within oneself all of the conflict one sees in the world. If one can take sides one can get some emotional catharsis out of conflicts, but if one identifies with both sides tremendous internal stress is liable to occur. And, in a neurotic state we feel compassion, thus we feel a lot of pain about the state of the world.

While I was non-judgemental that doesn't mean I wasn't critical of others. I was always critical of dishonesty and hypocrisy. I could accept that there were people in the world who raped, killed and tortured the innocent. I didn't see this as a good thing, but it was at least honest. But it seemed as if dishonesty and hypocrisy caused more suffering in the world than violence, especially since they often led to violence.

And this is what I mean when I talk about our tendency to project the disowned part of ourselves onto the world around us and then fight against it. The reason that the one thing in the world I couldn't stand was dishonesty was because my own dishonesty was the thing I was trying to disown. At the height of my neurosis I was going around being an idealistic do-gooder, working for an environmental organisation, but deep down I was just a pit of seething repressed hostility. My colleagues were praising me for my selflessness and generosity while my OCD was asking me whether they would still think so highly of me of I raped and killed their teenage daughter.

This is the nature of Obsessive Compulsive Disorder. Everyone I've come in contact with who has it is scrupulously considerate of others, polite and concerned about always doing the right thing. But at the same time plagued by thoughts about doing things like killing babies or putting puppies in the microwave.

How I've come out of that situation is through finding insight into myself and others, which I'm presenting in this book, and learning to express any repressed hostility through sick humour rather than keeping it bottled up. I think that the only reason that these hostile feelings build up for those of us who don't allow ourselves an outlet is because of an unhelpful framework of thinking about ourselves and the world. Once we have a framework which works, we feel little frustration and thus little hostility.

Sexuality

In discussing the nature of sexuality it is necessary to simplify things to a degree. There are qualities that we can reasonably associate with one gender or the other based on probability. The fact that Margaret Thatcher manifests a patriarchal mindset does not alter the fact that patriarchy is an expression of the masculine. Similarly it is helpful to speak about homosexuality without getting into the finer technicalities of Kinsey's sliding scale of sexual orientation. Homosexuality, like the masculine and the feminine, is something which exists in degrees of purity, but I think the fluidity inherent in the thesis I put forward here is consistent with that variability.

But first we need to examine what we mean by sex. We can forget about the role of sex for reproduction. There is nothing new that I can say about that. The mystery that needs to be explored is that of recreational sex. Why is it important to us? What do we get out of it? Why are the sexual desires of many, if not most, of us gender specific? And what determines to which gender we feel most attracted?

The non-reproductive sexual behaviour of humans exists along a sliding scale. At one end is what we can truly describe as the act of making love. At the other end is rape.

The act of making love is a physical union between equals characterised by the sharing of physical pleasure and in which all party's are paying full attention to the other participants. This definition allows for the possibility for an act of genuine lovemaking to include more than two participants, but I do feel that such an act is hard to achieve because it is hard to truly focus one's physical affections on more than one person at a time. Love divided is love diluted.

Next on the scale would be sexual acts in which one or both parties are not really concerned about the pleasure their partner is receiving as long as they are getting what they want or where one or both partners are thinking about someone other than the person with whom they are having sex. Love is still present here as long as one person is giving pleasure to another, but it is one way. It is important to emphasise that there is nothing wrong with this if the nature of the transaction is understood by both parties. Love is a healing force and the more we are unwell the more we need love. To gratefully accept the physical love of another person when we feel unable to fully return it is no different to accepting the care of doctors and nurses when we are in hospital.

Then there are sexual acts engaged in for financial reasons. The need for something that at least feels like love is here on the part of the purchaser, and a degree of genuine affection is by no means uncommon on the part of the provider, but this is clearly not on the same level as an act in which physical love is being freely given.

Then there are various kinds of sexual relationship which are coercive or exploitative. Mutually exploitative relationships needn't be destructive, for instance a prospective starlet having sex with a producer in return for a job is often an equal exchange in the same way that any form of prostitution can be an equal exchange. But if the situation is not one of equality it becomes true exploitation and is a destructive act. Accepting a blow job from a crack addict in return for some small change is an act devoid of love.

Love is a process of opening up, reaching out and seeking union. It is the opposite of repression or control. We long for wholeness within ourselves and we pursue that wholeness by embracing in the outside world that which corresponds to our suppressed self. Most of us men need to reconnect with the feminine part of ourselves that we have had to repress. So we seek loving union with women. But if we are too extremely neurotic to be able to open up to love, but rather fear the threat it poses to our ego's fixed state, we may repress our loving instincts further by turning the act of love into an act of violence and attacking the individual who might otherwise be seen as a love object by raping them.

But, if we began our lives by being bisexual as Freud asserts, how do we come to be fixated principally on one or the other gender? And what determines which gender it is?

First we have to return to the story of our origins.

We left off with the establishment of monogamy and sexual repression generally. From here the split between men and woman continued. The angrier and more insecure the men became the more they felt threatened by the women who represented their disowned selves. And the more insensitive the men's behaviour the more the women would criticise them and so on.

For a long time society remained matriarchal with the nurturers ultimately calling the shots. But as the men became more and more embattled and had to repress their original nature further and further down into their unconscious, they became more and more angry towards that nature and anything that might represent it in the outside world. This was the beginnings of misogyny. Men's anger at women, arising from their resentment that women could still live at peace with their instincts and be relatively happy while they themselves were in an embattled state of self-doubt, threatened to tear society apart. The only answer was a compromise. Men would not destroy women, but they demanded the right to enchain and control women in the same way that they had to enchain and control their original nature. As long as what was outside mirrored what was inside, psychological stability and thus the stability of society was possible. And a stable society was needed if we were to find understanding. The price that was paid, however, was enormous. Women, the nurturers of the children, were spiritually crippled by their enslavement and became nearly as unhappy and neurotic as the men.

This is the furnace within which our sexuality is forged. Our sexual desire is a pull toward wholeness. The man wants to experience loving acceptance from the original source of criticism of his newly aggressive and competitive behaviour. The woman wants man to come back to her. In her heart of hearts she is still sitting around that campfire looking in heartbreaking sadness at the man who has lost his soul fighting leopards. She wants to love away the pain.

Our sexual love object is a symbol for that with which we want to reunite inside ourselves. Men often are attracted to young pretty women. The features we identify as pretty are childlike features - slim build, wide eyes, full lips and smooth skin. Men's predilection for such women is so great that, over the process of a couple of a million years, it has led to us becoming more childlike in appearance as a species. We have lost most of our body hair as well as our sloping foreheads. The adult human looks remarkably like a chimpanzee foetus. The reason for this preference is that we associate youth with lack of neurosis, with innocence if you like, with a generosity of spirit, a uninhibited capacity for love. Of course what ignites our sexual arousal is here a symbol and may not reflect the psychological reality of the individual. There is also the MILF (mother I'd like to fuck) archetype. Here once again there is a desire to reunited with the instinct for love but now in the form of the nurturing mother.

One complaint that many men make is that women aren't attracted to nice guys. Of course this isn't true. Women's taste in sexual partners varies greatly. But the complaint arises because of the mystery that many women love men who are not good to them. And in the extreme we see the case of women falling in love with jailed serial killers. But this makes sense if we remember that the origins of modern sexuality are to be found in women's use of their sexuality as a way of soothing the aggression of men and thus re-socialising them. While the pleasurable sensations of sex can be reason enough to seek it out, it can also be an expression of our deeper selves, and since our deepest nature is one of unconditional love, the desire to use sex as a healing force is very strong in us.

Now we come to the mystery of homosexuality. Bisexuality was our original orientation. A focus of attraction on the opposite sex is explained above. But why do some of us move from bisexuality to an exclusive attraction to the same sex?

I believe the key here is patriarchy - the male-oriented society. Sexual love is driven by a desire to be welcomed back into that from which we feel we have been excluded or to welcome another back. For most of us this desired return is a return to the primal state. But a patriarchal social order has the potential to form another split within males. We can be doubly excluded. First we were excluded from the loving tribal family, now we can be excluded from the patriarchal brotherhood. Now I'm not suggesting that anyone who is not a man's man becomes a homosexual, far from it. In tribal societies some men did not pass the initiation ceremonies and remained living with the women, but they were not necessarily homosexual. What I'm suggesting is that the underlying reason for a man's fixation on sex with another man, as opposed to a propensity to be sexually attracted to either sex, is a deep unmet desire to be accepted into the brotherhood of men.

On the surface this idea seems ridiculous. For a start, having sex with other men is no way to gain acceptance into a social order that tends to despise homosexuals. Secondly, many homosexuals vehemently reject the patriarchal order. And thirdly, many homosexuals are accepted in the patriarchal order when they don't advertise their sexual preference.

But imagine you are a young boy. You want to fit in with the other lads, but for some reason they reject you. If you are very secure in yourself, perhaps you go your own way resigned but not fixated on the rejection. But if you are truly hurt by the rejection you may react in a number of ways : you may express your pain by mocking those who rejected you (essentially saying, "I didn't want a be a member of your club anyway!") ; you may become introverted, hiding your pain and trying to not be rejected further by outwardly conforming to the expectations of those who initially showed you signs of rejection ; or you may overcompensate by assuming a persona of super masculinity. This is what happens on the surface, but deep down, where your sexual drives lie, rejection by men has superseded rejection by women (and our original nature) as the rift that your sexuality longs to heal. Your psychological response to the original rejection may determine the type of men you want to make love to, but it is only a man who can answer your principle need for healing.

To clarify the different types of response :
1. Mocking those who reject you. One of the most common

forms this takes is flamboyant effeminacy. Since aggressive self-discipline is so important to the patriarchal order, to act in an effeminate and unrestrained manner, is an act of rebellion against that order.

2. Introversion. This is simply remaining in the closet, living in a miserable state of conformity lest you suffer further rejection.

3. Super masculinity. An obvious example is the macho leather-clad gays.

In recent times, with intolerance towards homosexuals still being rife, many look to biology to provide a rationale for tolerance. But this is a risky strategy. It is unlikely we will ever find a gay gene. Common sense suggests that such a gene would be self-eliminating anyway. If we rest our arguments on science and then science fails to come up with the desired result our position is seriously compromised. As for those who talk about a "cure for homosexuality", the best argument arising from my hypothesis, is that, if homosexual sex is therapy for childhood trauma, the only thing that might eventually change the homosexual's orientation would be having far more homosexual sex than he is at the moment.

As for lesbianism, that is fairly easy to understand. Men can be very difficult and loving them can be a painful process. Since the sexual drive is a drive toward wholeness, and the feminine, unlike the masculine, is not divided against itself, a woman does not need a man to find wholeness through sexuality.

The battle for sexual tolerance requires a strong and unequivocal stand. As long as we are careful not to do damage to ourselves or others, all sex is good for us. Sex can heal us. Sex can make us better people.

Acknowledging the neurotic roots of our sexual desires does not demean those desires, it ennobles them. And it ennobles us. We are not shameful deviants, as some like to claim. We are the wounded soldiers of society's struggle for self-knowledge taking the time to lick each other's wounds.

Sexual Fixations

As children we naturally were interested in finding out what feels good. (Even foetuses in the womb often discover the pleasure of masturbation.) But sometimes these forms of exploration would bring a negative response from adults.

If we got the message that some aspect of our behaviour was unacceptable, we might become fixated on it and carry this fixation into adult life. For example a little boy who wanted to see whether it felt good to put on his sister's dress and panties might meet with the censure of his parents and feel that he was unacceptable because he had carried out this experiment.

Like a sore tooth that we can't seem to stop poking with our tongue, the memory of rejection keeps us going back and re-enacting the moment, preferably in some context in which we can feel accepted. So the little boy, now a transvestite, will dress up as a woman in a community with others who do likewise, basking in a mutual show of acceptance of that which deep down they still do not fully accept.

Where this must be a particularly difficult problem is where the fixation is on something which can be genuinely destructive and thus carries a social taboo which is not merely intolerance of difference.

Such is the case with pedophilia. It is normal for a child to feel an erotic attraction to other children, but if we fixate on this kind of attraction in a way which causes us to carry it into adulthood then it becomes a serious problem, especially if we act on these feelings and, as a result, harm children.

Even in such a case the principle still applies that the past cannot be changed and that the thoughts and emotions are, in themselves, morally neutral, but the individual could not use the argument, as with the transvestite, that acting on the desire was harmless.

Luckily, for most of us, if we find ourselves fixated on

something it is something far easier for us to learn to accept and thus move on from.

This shouldn't be taken as meaning that sexual fetishes are necessarily a bad thing, only that they are a limiting thing. There are advantages in being able to enjoy a wider range of sexual experiences.

What is the Imagination?

Our mind has two basic modes of operation - reason and imagination.
Reason gathers information and applies logic to try to draw conclusions from it.
Imagination is the free operation of the mind unrestricted by reference to external reality.
Imagination serves a number of functions. Since the nature of the universe is such that patterns reoccur, patterns which are discovered by the free operation of the imagination may prove useful to the reason in making sense of similar patterns observed in the environment. This is what we call intuition. An example of this function of the imagination is the formation of myths. The story of Odysseus returning from the battle of Troy was no doubt built upon the seed of a real man's experience, but the imagination added details about witches and sirens and a cyclops. While these might have been created for sheer entertainment, they expressed patterns which resonated with aspects of individual human experience and the nature of the human journey in search of self-understanding. It is because of these resonances that the myth has been treasured over the centuries. But the imagination is inescapably prophetic. To the extent that it is allowed to depart from conventional paths it will symbolically express something significant about the individual and their society. This is why dreams, in which the mind's imagination is at its freest, are so open to rewarding interpretation. So imagination can be used for self-exploration also. And lastly it can be used in a directed sense to provide emotional compensation for things missing in our lives. If we feel frustrated and powerless we may fantasise about being Rambo. If we are unable to have the sexual experiences we long for we can experience them through fantasy. And imagination can also be an arena for healing in which we allow the separate parts of our being to have their own voice and find their way to reconciliation.

The Scary Side of the Imagination

When we allow the imagination to run free we may find that it throws up some frightening ideas.

In our repressed, i.e. armoured, state we repress most of our angry feelings and much of our sexuality. So when the imagination wanders off the safe path of our disciplined ways of thinking about ourselves, it is bound to bump into aggressive and sexual images and thoughts. The higher our standards of behaviour, the more of these things we will find. We all experience frustration when things don't go our way. Either we express ourselves angrily or we repress those hostile feelings. Likewise, we all have erotic feelings. Since our original sexuality was unstructured, these feelings won't necessarily be limited to those that fit with our concept of proper behaviour for a person of our sexual orientation. We try to live out any sexual feelings we feel are appropriate. It is the inappropriate feelings which get repressed. So finding thoughts in our imagination which we might consider to be depraved or monstrous, is not an indication that we are depraved or monstrous, but an indication that we are not. A depraved or monstrous individual would have done those things.

What can make these thoughts particularly scary is that they tend to crystallise lots of repressed feelings into something extreme. So restraining ourselves from punching someone in the nose, if repeated twenty times, might crystallise in our imagination as a thought of taking a machine gun and committing mass murder. And repressed anger and sexuality could cross-fertilise into violent sexual fantasies.

As I mentioned earlier, one of the thoughts that arose unbidden in my mind which gave me the most trouble was that of killing a baby. Clearly I had been repressing a lot of anger at the time. My conscience was particularly oppressive, so this is likely.

But the solution to this problem is to learn to accept that even terrible thoughts are only thoughts. Humour can be very helpful in achieving this. Now I can imagine playing football and using an infant as a ball. This is so ludicrous that it makes me realise the difference between thoughts and actions.

Degrees of Being Alive

A living system is characterised by the free flow of materials, information and energy and an efficient spontaneous interaction with the environment. In our bodies, blood flows constantly, a constant stream of information is carried through our nervous system, oxygen flows into the body and waste products flow out. And we interact relatively spontaneously with our environment. If someone throws a ball at our head we either duck or try to catch it. When we are dead, these flows will not occur, and our body will not respond to its environment. If you throw a ball at a corpse, you'll hit it quite easily as long as your aim is good.

While some of us may be affected by ailments which impede our full efficiency as a living system, there is only minor variation in the aliveness of our bodies, until we are dead.

It seems fair to apply this same concept of aliveness to our emotional and intellectual selves. Here we find a great deal of variation in states of aliveness depending on how armoured we are.

Character armour impedes the free flow of ideas in the mind, and body armour impedes the free flow of emotion. Dogmatic, stereotypical forms of thinking keep the mind closed down and interfere with the individual's ability to think clearly and respond to evidence that might challenge preconceived ideas. And body armour deadens the organism's capacity for bodily sensation - this includes the relief that comes with cathartic expressions of sorrow, joy or anger, as well as the sensory pleasure which can come from the apprehension of visual or aural beauty, the taste of delicious food or the ecstasy of erotic sex.

And, when armouring is in place, the individual cannot interact truly spontaneously with their environment. Much concentration is needed to maintain the armouring and this concentration is not available for acknowledging outside factors. And the armoured individual can only respond within the bounds of their stereotyped behaviour. To get an idea of the disadvantages of character and body armour, imagine a team of mediaeval knights in full body armour trying to play a game of football.

It is said that most of us only use 10% of our brain's capacity. This is because our thinking is impeded by our character armour. Since thinking truthfully would destroy our armoured ego structure, we have to spend a huge amount of our intellectual ability on finding ways to function *without* thinking truthfully.

A good example of this is the theory in evolutionary biology which interprets human behaviour in terms of the genes need to reproduce. (See *The Moral Animal : Why We Are the Way We Are : The New Science of Evolutionary Psychology* by Robert Wright (Vintage, 1995).) Unable to think truthfully and acknowledge that we are suffering psychologically and that self-directed awareness is the natural response of an organism to suffering, some of us had to find another way to explain (i.e. justify) this aspect of our behaviour. But if one tries to explain human behaviour by reference to animal behaviour in this way one ends up with a complex unwieldy theory which strives to explain everything from Shakespeare writing his plays to the Pope wearing a ridiculously large hat as outgrowths of the genes' struggle to proliferate. It takes a huge amount of intellectual effort to build and maintain such a complex alternative to admitting that we have become sick. And, of course, the only individuals who pay any attention to such ridiculous theories are intellectuals.

So it is not unfair to speak of the armoured individual as being less alive than the un-armoured individual, if we judge aliveness in terms of sensory awareness, freedom of thought and capacity for spontaneous interaction with others and the environment.

I'm not a religious person, so I don't believe in a life for the ego after physical death. But I look for associations and patterns where I can find them. And it has struck me that a lot of what Jesus is quoted as having said about life after death and not having to die, would make a lot of sense if what was being referred to was not physical death, but the living death of armoured existence, especially given the emphasis he placed on sin (i.e. selfishness) as being a problem to be solved and forgiveness (i.e. acceptance) as key to that solution. I wouldn't claim that this is what he was talking about. It may simply be another example of the way in which the systematic nature of life and the universe is manifested in repeated patterns.

Depression

When we are depressed we are cut off from reality, trapped within the tiny world of our own withdrawn ego. This is a bit of a paradox. If reality were an unpleasant place and we withdrew into our own ideal dream world, that might make sense. But reality is a beautiful place and when we are depressed we retreat from it into a place which is truly horrible. Why?

Thoughts are the body of the ego, whether it is a free ego thinking spontaneously and laterally, or an obsessed ego running around in circles.

Though it has many variants, the central thought of the depressed mind is, "I'm a bad person." This thought makes us think that we deserve to be cut off from the beauty of reality and, ironically, our attempts to fight our way back out again are what keep us where we are. We become like the man who is so anxious to escape the burning building through the revolving door that he runs too fast and ends up constantly revolving back in again.

What keeps us cut off from healing reality is that we keep thinking about ourselves. There is a simple trick we might try to short-circuit this process. If we fear that we may be a worthless individual, then we might ask ourselves : "How bad would it be if that were the case?" What would it mean if we had no worth? Nothing could be expected of us. The world would not cease to exist. We would still be capable of experiencing pleasure. To be worthless would simply be to be insignificant or unimportant. (Of course this isn't the same as being bad, but it is still worth a try.)

If we can accept that, even if we were worthless, it would not be such a bad thing, then we can stop the self-justification merry-go-round that keeps us cut off from our capacity for unconditional love. Our inner child is capable of loving us unconditionally as much as anyone else.

There are two major kinds of depression - reactive and endogenous. Reactive depression is depression which is triggered by an outside event. This could include the break-up of a relationship, a death in the family or giving birth. Endogenous depression seems to originate spontaneously without an outside trigger.

Given that the central thought of depression is "I am a bad person" we can see that the most likely cause for endogenous depression is self-condemnation based on "sick" ideas formed from repressed emotions. Very often those most prone to depression are those whose behaviour is impeccable. So why should such individuals come to believe that they are bad? The well-behaved person is someone who represses any antisocial impulses. This means that the subconscious of the well-behaved individual is more likely to contain "evil" thoughts. Not realising that the existence of such thoughts is a sign of moral rectitude rather than the opposite, the endogenous depressive condemns himself when he comes in contact with such thoughts.

One of my early depressive episodes, as I've mentioned, was exacerbated by the thought of killing a baby. Such a thought is a fairly typical one for the individual who keeps a very tight reign on his anger. When we are feeling unhappy it makes us selfish. A new baby gets all the attention, so we feel jealous. Our mind throws up the idea, "If I killed that baby, then they would pay attention to me." It is just a passing thought fired off by the brain. But the conscience comes into play. The conscience, as I've said, is another part of the ego which contains our ideas of right and wrong. The conscience condemns us for such a though. We try to think of some way of proving we are not really bad, but even the best defence is, in itself, a jail cell, because it is thinking obsessively about ourselves which keeps us cut off from the healing power of our deeper unconditionally loving self.

With reactive depression the process is exactly the same. It is not the event which triggers the depression which is really important to understanding it. What is important is understanding that the event leads the individual to feel that they are a bad person. In the case of a relationship break-up, "If I'm a good person, why did she dump me?" In the case of a death there is no doubt some regret involved for the person who becomes depressed, "If only I'd been a better son," or whatever. In the case of postnatal depression, there are two possible kinds of negative thought, "What a bad, screwed up person I am when I compare myself to a healthy, unspoilt infant!" and/or "I'm not a good enough person to be responsible for the care of this precious child."

Some claim that depression is all a matter of brain chemistry. While it may be true that the stress of depression brings about changes in the chemistry of the brain, from a close examination of the way that the obsessional thinking characteristic of depression keeps us trapped within ourselves and cut off from the healing potential of spontaneous and open communication with other people and the world around us, we can see that there are better approaches to releasing ourselves from depression than swallowing pills or having epileptic seizures induced by the application of electricity to our brains. These things have provided a limited amount of help to some individuals, including myself, but they are really the equivalent of providing air-conditioning in the prison cell instead of unlocking the door.

Self-Acceptance and a Troubled World

There are many problems in the world which often seem insoluble - ecological collapse, poverty, war, political oppression and disease, to name some of the obvious ones.

Many have made a great effort to fight these problems, but, at times, it seems futile. As with depression, sometimes it seems as if the more we try to do something about the problem the worse it gets.

Psychology is a huge factor in these problems.

The key factor in our ecological problems is consumption, whether of food, manufacturing materials, living space or energy. Population is also crucial. It's a case of how many of us there are and how much we are using of which resources. Our basic physical needs are, for most of us, a very small subset of what we consume. Our psychological needs determine most of our consumption. And, similarly, how many offspring we have is a psychological decision, unless the condom broke.

Poverty is a symptom of a malfunctioning social system in which the basic physical needs of some are not met because the resources which could meet those needs are being directed towards satisfying the psychological needs of others.

So ecological problems and poverty are highly dependent on consumption, and this is something which varies according to our psychological needs. I'm not saying we should strive to consume less. But when we are armoured we can't get as much enjoyment out of the things that we have and therefore we need more. And we are less flexible in what we chose to consume. Materialism is a poor substitute for other more social forms of enjoyment. When we are not locked up within ourselves we will find that we can have more fun interacting with others - partying, creating, having sex - than we can polishing our trophies. When we felt worthless, our possessions told us that we were not, but when we no longer feel that way, we will have little use for many of them.

While there may be many specific contributing factors to war the underlying driving force is neurosis. The desire to use violence to change the behaviour of others is a symptom of a divided self. To directly protect ourselves when attacked is a natural function of the healthy organism. And it is natural to feel anger when we are treated unjustly. But to believe that we can improve our lot in life by invading Poland, that killing people in a foreign land will make us safer at home or that we can free ourselves from an oppressively hierarchical global political structure by flying planes into the economic centre of the nation at its peak, are irrational conclusions driven by the divided individual's need to find a target for his or her self-contempt. But, even if one does not accept this assessment, one has to admit that someone who is not in a healthy psychological state is not going to make good decisions in an activity as dangerous and prone to backfiring as waging war.

Political oppression is something which is only easy to maintain when the confidence of the majority of members of your society is compromised by internal psychological division. Tyrants may resort to murder and torture, but they are always outnumbered when the population doesn't consist mainly of individual's predisposed to submission. Wilhelm Reich, in his book *The Mass Psychology of Fascism* (Farrar, Straus and Giroux, 1933), put forward the theory that the phenomenon of Naziism could only occur in a society which was sexually repressive. If there is some part of ourselves which we are not accepting then this makes us vulnerable to manipulation and intimidation. This is also something which is understood by many leaders of religious cults. Encourage an individual crying out for acceptance to feel ashamed of masturbating or desiring material goods and you can get them to do anything.

Great progress is being made in fighting disease, but it is still with us. Now I would not claim that the emotional benefits of self-acceptance are going to cure diseases. But how well our bodily system can fight a curable disease or cope with an incurable one depends on how well it is functioning. And the repression of emotion through bodily armouring places immense stress on the body and decreases its ability to deal with problems. And there is evidence that mood plays a tremendous role in making us susceptible to some diseases and affecting our ability to combat them. There is much anecdotal evidence of "faith healing". While this can be a popular con job practised in some religions, in other cases the results appear to be genuine. Where this does occur the key is clearly not some magical intervention by a cosmic spirit, but evidence of the role of expectation on physical ailments in some individuals. In a case discussed by Laurens van der Post in his book *About Blady : A Pattern Out of Time - A Memoir* (Morrow, 1991), the faith was faith in a surgeon, rather than a deity. A doctor did an exploratory operation on a peasant and found him to be riddled with cancer. All he could do was sow him up again. But the peasant thought the doctor, who very much impressed him, must have removed the cancer. When the doctor returned to the village a number of years later he found his patient still alive and now cancer free. And Wilhelm Reich, who believed that emotional and sexual repression caused cancer and that sitting in one of his orgone accumulators could cure it, found that it worked for some of his patients. Once again the results were probably due to the patient's faith in Reich rather than the effectiveness of his accumulators. The placebo effect, in which some patients get better when given a sugar pill and told that it is medicine, is another example. The point is that, while a positive state of mind may not cure an illness, it isn't going to hurt.

The other factor in dealing with all of these problems is our ability to co-operate. When armoured our ability to work together on problem-solving is limited. In our insecure state we are prone to find ourselves in conflict with others and the process can be frustrating. But in the non-armoured state, not only are we able to co-operate in problem-solving, it becomes the most enjoyable activity imaginable. What we really want is to be in a state of loving communion with others. We strive for something like this at parties by getting together when relaxed and maybe reducing our inhibitions with some alcohol. The results are pretty variable. But the point is that, in the un-armoured state, we are in a state of loving communion with our friends all of the time regardless of what activity we are engaged in. Life, even a life of problem-solving, becomes a non-stop party.

Emotional Scars

Often we will have an experience which will leave us with painful feelings long after it is over in a physical sense. But if that experience was inflicted on us by a person who is no longer present or the result of a situation we are no longer in, then that individual or situation is no longer the source of our suffering. We are suffering because of the nature of our thinking about that event. We are torturing ourselves for no good reason, since the past cannot be changed.

We can see that the emotional scars inflicted by an experience are not based on how painful it was. I once lay strapped in a hospital bed begging the doctors and nurses to kill me. I felt that the whole of human history was going to come to nothing and that it was all my fault. I can't imagine much more intense psychological suffering than what I went through then, but that memory holds no pain for me now. That experience is in the past.

But if we are caught up in "if only" thoughts or self-recrimination, then we can prolong our suffering indefinitely.

An example of this might be if a guy left his baby to play unsupervised on the front lawn and it crawled out into traffic and was killed. The trauma of this is liable to be greater than if the baby were killed when a car crashed into the back of the car the father was driving. The death of the child is the same, but in one case the father is liable to blame himself, in the other case less so. Similarly, if a girl is raped, how much psychological suffering she experiences afterwards may depend on whether she thinks of herself as a victim or a survivor.

But in all cases the past in still the past. It can't be changed. Feelings of recrimination or regret are not required, but are almost certain to occur all the same. Like all emotions and thoughts they are best accepted. Thoughts ask only to be thought and feelings ask only to be felt. The path to letting go of them is to not fight them.

Compassion is Projected Self-Pity

As neurotic armoured individuals we are still able to connect with the suffering of others by identifying it with our own suffering in some way. In our suffering state our attention is directed towards ourselves, but, if we can identify our suffering with that of someone else it can motivate us to try to do something to help them and by feeling a sense that our suffering is shared we can achieve some sense of catharsis.

Since, in our neurotic armoured state our inner child is frightened, unloved, oppressed, starved, molested, blind, deaf and crippled, there are few forms of suffering in the world with which we are incapable of identifying.

Clearly in a neurotic society compassion, the ability to feel identification with another's suffering, is tremendously important as it allows for mutual aid between pathologically self-centred individuals.

However, as we become less neurotic and thus suffer less ourselves we may be worried about the fact that we start to feel less compassion for others. If we express to others the fact that seeing people suffer on the news each night no longer makes us feel bad, they may tell us that there is something wrong with us. But this is actually a sign of increasing mental health.

Some incredibly armoured individuals feel no compassion for others. We call them sociopaths. These are not healthy individuals. They are totally self-centred and very often behave very destructively towards others. Their lack of compassion is not due to a state of health, but to the fact that their armouring is so complete that it blocks out all awareness of their inner child's suffering.

The end of compassion, however, does not mean the end of mutual aid buts its true beginning. When we are no longer at war with ourselves we will be full of energy and enthusiasm, and the most enjoyable way of using that energy is in helping others. It is not necessary for us to be motivated by an experience of their pain any more than it is necessary for us to be dirty ourselves in order to feel motivated to clean the kitchen floor.

The Inner Child

While it is true that, in our neurotic state, our inner child suffers greatly, we need to understand that the inner child is not vulnerable in the way that a real child is vulnerable. Nothing can ever kill or injure the inner child in any way. Our scars are a part of our neurotic ego, our inner child, suffer as it may, can never be scarred.

The essence of the inner child (or our original nature) is unconditional love. We are capable of feeling love that does not depend on the behaviour or nature of the one loved. And this capacity is a function of our inner child.

When we are neurotic, not understanding the nature of the inner child, it is easy for us to feel paranoid, to feel that the inner child judges us harshly for oppressing it. Once again there is the phenomenon of projection. We can assume that the guilt that we feel, the lack of self-acceptance, has its origin in the inner child rather than in the fragility of the neurotic ego structure itself. And, in some cases, we may project aspects of our own state onto that which we have disowned and thus see the inner child as something evil and malicious.

These phenomena account for a tendency in our society for some individuals to feel a fear of children or a hostility towards them. Culturally we have evil child horror movies such as *The Omen* which reflect this fear. And in religion the concept of original sin projects our awareness of our own selfish nature onto the blank slate of the new born child. And, in the extreme, we have individuals whose fear of their own inner child, and their belief that it may condemn them, drives them to torture, kill or molest children.

All of this is based on a lack of understanding that the inner child is incapable of condemnation. Love is not unconditional if it carries with it any capacity for value judgement. Condemnation and value judgements are functions of the neurotic ego.

Since the voice of the inner child is the un-warped expression of the natural processes of the universe as manifested in the organised form of matter we call humanity, the voice of the inner child is the voice of what religious people call "God". In the Christian religion we can see this reflected in the concept that God tells us that we are sinful (i.e. selfish) but he loves us anyway. This is nothing more than what our own deepest self has been trying to tell us all along.

So the concept of self-acceptance is not just a gimmick to make us feel better, it is reunion with our deepest instinctive self and a realisation of the promises embodied in our religions that we would some day find salvation from our state of suffering and re-enter paradise. The whole of human history has been little more than an ultimately easily cured state of insanity.

In the Christian religion, much that is said about The Kingdom of Heaven also applies to a non-neurotic global society. The problem with this term is that "kingdom" implies submission to a higher power as we have in neurotically hierarchical forms of social organisation and "heaven" implies that it takes place on some otherworldly plane of existence. Never-the-less, if one ignores the inappropriate name, much of what Jesus said about this state and how it might come about seems very appropriate.

What is Consciousness?

We experience our lives. We think our thoughts. We have our feelings. But what or who is the "we" that experiences these things?

We have a body. We have a mind. We have an ego structure or personality. These give structure to our experience. They are media through which we experience.

We might think of these aspects of ourselves as a musical instrument. But what is the nature of the music itself?

Thinking is the construction and manipulation of patterns of information. But, we can stop thinking (i.e. stop processing or manipulating information) and still be conscious. This is what the discipline of meditation is all about.

Nor are the five senses necessary to consciousness. Even if we were to remove our ability to see, hear, taste, feel or smell, we would still be aware of the fact that we existed. We might know we existed because of our thought processes, but, once again, we could cease to think and still be aware of raw, unstructured, unmediated consciousness.

So what is this consciousness?

Thought takes place through the communication of information through the synapses in our brain. And physical awareness is possible because of the transmission of information through the nervous system generally. These are the conduits for our consciousness - they give it its shape - but what is it that is travelling through these conduits?

The answer is energy - the raw stuff of the universe.

Now we have to take a massive, seemingly insane leap and ask "What if energy itself is conscious? What if our consciousness, our awareness, the raw stuff of our experience, is nothing more than energy's awareness of its own existence?"

This may seem like madness, but if we take some time to consider it, we will find that :

a. We can't disprove it. We can't prove that unstructured energy or inanimate objects have no awareness. We can observe that these things do not act like living organisms. But that proves nothing. Even with living beings, behaviour can give us clues about the experience or awareness of the being, but we don't know what consciousness looks like, even if it looks like anything at all. So we have no reliable way of detecting it.

b. If we accept the concept that consciousness is energy's self-awareness as a provisional hypothesis we can see that some otherwise inexplicable phenomena actually begin to make some kind of sense.

First it is important to understand what is not being suggested here, which is that energy or inanimate objects have thoughts or feelings. Thoughts and feelings are structured forms of consciousness which are most likely restricted to living things, as they are dependent on some kind of nervous system. But what flows through these structures is energy.

We have emotions. The word contains the word "motion" because emotions are characterised by flow. When we feel an emotion it is the sensation of energy moving through the structure of our ego in some way. In anger, the energy explodes through cracks in the armour of the ego structure or threatens to do so. We feel it simmering. In sorrow we feel emotion flowing through us perhaps expressed through sobs and tears. We feel pain when the free flow of energy in our body is hampered by damage of some kind.

The phenomenon of orgasm is a good way of looking at the nature of our consciousness. While, for the male, the ejaculation of seminal fluid is not always accompanied by the ecstatic experience we think of as characterising the orgasm, nevertheless, we know what we mean by the orgasmic experience. How does this happen? What makes this bodily experience so appealing to us. It is not simply the expelling of a bodily substance. That happens when we sneeze or take a shit. We might be relieved but we do not have a heavenly experience.

Wilhelm Reich, who developed the concepts of body armour

and character armour, found that these forms of armouring may be temporarily broken down by the bodily experience of orgasm. This allows energy to flow far more freely in the body for a brief period of time.

So we see that the emotional or bodily experience which allows for our most intense experiences of bliss is one in which energy flows freely through our body, and that pain accompanies the hindering of that flow, by disease or injury or armouring.

Remember when you were a young child and you felt blissfully happy running through an open field? Why? You were just running. It was just a field. What's the big deal? The big deal is that you felt free. You weren't hemmed in or frustrated. You were energy expressing the nature of energy.

But this doesn't mean that we want freedom from structure altogether. We want to feel energy flow freely through our bodies, but we don't want to spontaneously combust. Creativity occurs when the free flow of information or energy finds a form which makes possible something which didn't previously exist. So the healthy growth of individuals and societies is what feels best to them. The system of organisation of the individual or society is not oppressive in itself, but only becomes so if it is faulty in some way.

When we feel motivated or creative we say that we are filled with enthusiasm. What do we mean by "enthusiasm"? The literal meaning of the term is "the god within". Since our concept of God is a personification that we place upon the creative principle of the universe - energy and its intrinsic potential for orderly creative organisation - then we can see that the enthusiasm or spirit or soul which lives within us and is the very substance of our experience - is "God" operating through us. And this "God" is essentially self-aware energy. We are "God".

Because, in our armoured state, we are so used to thinking of ourselves as isolated, largely unconnected entities, this is bound to seem a crazy idea. But if we think of ourselves as robots all plugged into the same power supply it may make more sense. Also we might think of somebody suffering from multiple personality disorder. They are physically one person, and they began with one personality, but once that personality has split, each new personality experiences itself as different and generally in conflict with the others. Of course we don't share a single body, but the deeper we go into ourselves the more we discover that our concept of our self as separate is an illusion.

Love is the awareness of the connectedness between us. In essence love is a form of communication. Most of the time we are shut up within our armour, but, when we feel less vulnerable and drop our armour to some extent, we feel the pull of our oneness, the pull towards the unification of the whole. The reason we think of love in terms of specific relationships - parent and child or in a romantic relationship or marriage - is because these are special situations in which we either feel relaxed enough to drop our armour or feel the need or appropriateness of doing so, as in the case of caring for a child. But we can feel love for anyone if we drop our armour and doing so is a powerful encouragement for them to do likewise. Now that we can understand these things, armour will fast become a thing of the past and we will discover that the bliss of love which we only tasted infrequently before will become the very essence of our day to day experience.

We can also understand now our concepts about life after death. Fear of death is essentially fear that the ego is impermanent. Our ego is our concept of who we are. In the armoured state, we feel very anxious, because our ego structure is fragile. And we know that it will not last forever. At some point our body will die.

First we have to understand that the ego does not necessarily survive until we die. We can suffer a nervous breakdown followed by reintegration of parts of our character or change the whole orientation of our ego - for instance in the case of some people who become born again to a religion - and thus we are not really the same people as we were even though we haven't yet died. The same could be said about someone whose personality changes due to a painful illness or dementia. The ego is, by its nature, impermanent.

But, even if our ego survives to physical death, it won't survive beyond it. With the body goes any remnants of the structure which made us who we are.

However, if the essence of our consciousness lies in energy and its experience of its flow, then we can see that the essence of existence will remain. Energy can never be destroy virtually by definition. Only the structures within which the energy flows can be destroyed. So the concept put forward by some mystics that death means the merging of our consciousness with the universe seems valid.

We can see that the concept of self-aware energy animating our existence is compatible with the concept of the soul.

A couple of distinctions have to be made here though. Some see the soul as being specific to the person and surviving the death of the person in a separate form. If we are going to call the self-aware energy of the universe "the soul", then we have to acknowledge that it is a collective soul. What makes us separate entities is the experience of physical containment in the body and, more importantly, our armouring, which is an accumulation of emotional scars.

Even the very concept of ourselves as a separate continuing thing is an illusion. We are a pattern through which flows an ever changing assortment of matter and the energy of the universe taken in through the food we eat, the light of the sun, heat, etc., etc. We are always in flux. And the pattern survives only as long as it is viable.

It is also very important to distinguish between the soul and the conscience. The soul has no morality. A serial killer is an expression of the soul just as much as a saint. The creative process of the universe is an improvisation. There are inherent potentials which manifest themselves, but there is no overreaching intelligence to guide the process. Some paths lead on to bigger and healthier subsystems, and others are dead ends. We can see this in evolution. Some sea creature walked onto land and it was a success. The full potential of life on land was unleashed. But the dinosaurs proved to be a dead end.

The same self-aware energy is the motivating force behind the successes and the failures. Thus those who enacted the

Holocaust were full of genuine enthusiasm, but it was misdirected by their armouring into mass slaughter.

When it comes to how we act, we are influenced by a number of factors :

1. All else being equal we will avoid behaviour which causes us pain and pursue behaviour which makes us feel pleasure.

2. We may also allow reason to effect our behaviour. We may choose a course of action which involves pain if we reason that it confers an advantage for us in the long run.

3. In the armoured (i.e. divided) state, we may feel compelled to behave in a way which will allow us to not be rejected or otherwise badly treated by others. This is a form of avoidance of pain, but it becomes complex as we trade off different kinds of pain against each other.

4. Our conscience may influence our behaviour by making us feel guilty if we behave in a particular way. The conscience is a part of the ego - a part of our armouring - in which we store our expectations about ourselves. These are imparted to us socially and laid down as a part of the deeper structure of our personality. It may consist of codes of behaviour taught to us by our parents or our teachers and can incorporate ideas absorbed later in life from others if those ideas mesh in some way with what has already been laid down.

All of these ways of choosing our behaviour carry with them their own flaws and limitations. The first is very short term decision-making. Eating sweets may give me pleasure, but if I don't moderate that in the light of knowledge of the physical effects I'll make myself sick. The second is a very good approach but it is limited by our current understanding of the situation and may in some cases be too slow, as we can't always gather all the facts before making a decision. The long-term effectiveness of the third would depend on whether the majority were going in the most potentially successful direction. This may be the case after a problem has been solved, but if there is a major problem it is usually because the majority are going in the wrong direction. Also, it is fear-driven, and being intimidated into a course of action contaminates the health of the system. The fourth is once again effected by the accuracy of the absorbed ideas, but also, because the system is guilt-driven, it discourages rational examination of those ideas and being correction through intimidation leads to an unhealthy system.

Now we have the advantage of being able to integrate aspects of each approach into something which works more effectively. We are still going to want to seek pleasure and avoid pain. If these new ways of understanding ourselves and the universe are well-founded they will make it much easier for us to use reason as a guiding force in our behaviour. And we will be guided by others (although aware that at base we are all one), but only in the spirit of co-operation, and not through any sense of fear. And we will carry with us ideas about how to chose the kind of behaviour which is in the long-term interests of ourselves and the system of which we are a part but without any form of emotional oppression.

Impasses to Thought

If you think that what I say here makes sense and you wonder why you haven't come across these kinds of ideas before it is because the evolution of ideas, like the evolution of species, is obstructed by impasses.

For a long time animals only lived under the sea. The land represented a great opportunity for the flourishing of life, but fish were suited to life under the sea not to life on land. I don't know what lead to the first fish developing the ability to spend some of its time on land, but once it was there there were opportunities for new variations which, if successful, could proliferate and diversify and make full use of the terrestrial environment. When that first fish crawled up onto land it bridged a significant impasse. Similarly when we humans developed the ability for complex reasoning we bridged an impasse inherent in the limiting effects of the survival imperative and competition for mating opportunities in other species. Once that impasse was bridged we gradually took over the world.

Ideas develop in a similar way to animal species. We have ideas and if they seem useful others adopt them. Particularly powerful ideas which seem to be useful descriptions of aspects of the world take hold and become dominant. Then somebody comes up with a variation on one of those ideas, the thinking equivalent of a species mutation. Whether that idea takes off and leads to new ideas or perishes quickly depends on how well it fits either the needs of the society or the information that has been gathered about the world. Some ideas, like the theory of gravity, take hold because they are an effective description of observable reality and are useful in that way. Other ideas, such as the idea that behaving badly can lead to an eternity of pain in Hell, take hold because they effectively serve a social function, in this case control of antisocial behaviour.

So there is a survival of the fittest amongst ideas. Some ideas, such as that the sun revolves around the earth, die off when a more accountable explanation comes along.

But in the development of ideas there are also impasses. Of course in science we can be held back by the technological limits on gathering of information in our era. But, in broader philosophical thinking and in the development of a big picture framework for our scientific knowledge we can be held back by a fear of allowing ourselves to think certain thoughts.

In religious thinking we have the concept of blasphemy. While this doesn't directly effect philosophical or scientific thinking it is important to realise that religious thinking has had a tendency to have a big influence on acceptance of even scientifically valid ideas. Darwin was fearful about publishing his work on evolution because of the effect that it would have on people's religious beliefs, and, even today, some religious individuals resist accepting its validity.

But for the non-religious thinker there are still taboos. For an atheistic scientist any thought that might be leading him in the direction of acknowledging something that looks like God might be a taboo. And there are sexual taboos. Any re-examination of the nature of human sexuality can lead the individual to come up against those. And there is our natural fear of committing hubris. If our reason or intuition tells us we should turn the whole history of human thought on its head we may wonder who we are to do such a thing and we may doubt our own sanity.

The thoughts that can lead us to a concept of the world and ourselves that appears to work can include ones which we feel that we dare not even contemplate lest they lead us down a path to madness or irredeemable depravity. But once the impasse has been breached and those thoughts have been thought, then sometimes all the pieces of the picture rush together.

In my case, my mind was liberated by madness. I feared insanity, but I ended up there anyway, and, by good luck, it didn't kill me. And, as the psychiatrist R. D. Laing pointed out, breakdown can also be breakthrough. During my psychotic episodes my mind broke every taboo and committed every blasphemy. Caution was not an option. I had no control over my own mind. But when I returned to sanity, the impasses had been breached. I could travel back through those previously forbidden pathways if it were required to piece together a consistent explanation for my experiences and what I perceived about human behaviour generally.

Fight Against Only
That Which You Wish to Become

Since the purpose of our armouring is to protect us it stands to reason that criticism or hostility towards the armoured individual will generally be an ineffective approach to getting them to change their behaviour. Anything which makes them feel less secure will reinforce their armouring.

Very often when discussing things with those who cling to rigid dogmas, I've tried to point out that that dogmatic thinking is irrational or illogical in some way. I can't ever remember a case of them giving consideration to this criticism, rather, in most cases, they would respond simply by strongly restating their faith in that dogma. This makes sense, because dogma is precisely a defence against the brain's capacity for free thought based on the fear that such thought might lead to a scary place.

The way that things change for the better in the world is not through fighting against what is wrong but by developing an alternative to it. A good example of this is the intolerance of some conservative societies to some forms of sexuality. Such intolerance is not gone. In some societies it is still dominant. But if we look at what happened in countries like the United Kingdom and the United States where homosexuality was considered socially unacceptable by the majority of the population and sometimes illegal throughout the first half of the Twentieth Century, we will see that what brought about the change to the relatively more tolerant attitude we have today was not criticism of the conservative viewpoint, although that certainly occurred. What changed things was that a few individuals openly defied social expectation. When those who were still "living in the closet" saw the example being set and that those who were being true to themselves, while still treated appallingly in some cases, were, in general, happier than those, like themselves, who were giving in to social oppression, they began to follow that example. It is always hardest for the first individuals who break free of oppression. The more who pour through the crack that has opened in the dam of the dogmatic society, the easier it is for them all. Those who oppose homosexuality were once powerful individuals who could crush and kill the brightest in society as happened to Oscar Wilde, now they are just pathetic individuals waving placards at AID's victims funerals. That happened not through fighting them, but by refusing to be intimidated by them and showing that a life free of sexual repression could be a happier and more productive one.

While criticism and other forms of attack rarely bring about positive change in those whose behaviour is destructive, we also have to consider the danger that, in fighting against them, we are liable to become more like them.

During the Second World War, Great Britain fought against the Nazis in Germany and the Fascists in Italy. Now the Nazis were an example of a group of individuals who were so severely neurotically armoured that they had developed such a powerful fear of certain racial groups (and certain other groups) that they felt threatened as long as those individuals were present and so tried to exterminate them. Such an unhealthy society would, at some time, have to implode, but it was very efficient at killing people, so it had the capacity to take millions of innocent individuals with it on its path to self-destruction. And that is what it did.

But what happened when Great Britain fought a war against this horrific evil? Germany was in the thrall of a charismatic leader who was unquestioningly followed. So Great Britain got its own charismatic leader - Winston Churchill. Germany instituted state censorship and engaged in extensive propaganda. Great Britain instituted state censorship and engaged in extensive propaganda. Germany armed its young men and trained them to become effective killers. Great Britain armed its young men and trained them to be effective killers. Germany carried out the wholesale slaughter of civilians through the bombing of cities. Great Britain carried out the wholesale slaughter of civilians through the bombing of cities.

This does not mean that the fight against Naziism was wrong.

In a world in which neurotic armouring is the norm, you have to do whatever you can when a society starts carrying out an act of genocide.

The point is that the price we pay for that approach to fighting evil is that we become contaminated by it ourselves. We may not sink the the depths of our enemies but we follow them a good deal of the way.

Another example of this is the behaviour of some of those who fought against communism in the United States during the height of the Cold War. During the McCarthyist period individuals were fighting against communism by instituting censorship, jailing dissidents, encouraging citizens to inform on their neighbours and promoting patriotism, i.e. the submission of the individual to the concept of a collective state. And yet, surely, these were some of the very things which were wrong with communism.

Violence is Admission of Error

Facing the truth about ourselves can be very painful, although only if we don't have the correct framework of understanding. Hopefully, it has been made clear by now that our essential nature is a healthy one and that, to the extent that we may behave in an unhelpful way either to ourselves or others, this is due to unfounded ways of thinking about ourselves. The truth, once properly understood, sets us free.

Anger is what occurs when we become aware of a chink in our armour. Imagine you are defending a castle. What happens when someone tries to climb in through a window? That's when you pull out your gun and try to shoot them. Anger is like that.

Or you could think of it in terms of a volcanic eruption. The earth's tectonic plates are like our armouring. Where there is a weakness is where the magma can spew forth in an eruption.

This doesn't mean that anger is a bad thing. Like every emotion it is trying to lead us to wholeness. It needs to be felt, and, where possible, healthily expressed.

We can tell something about the truthfulness of an individual's belief system by observing their behaviour. A belief system which is logically consistent with observable reality is very stable and requires little effort or discipline to maintain. By contrast, a deluded belief system, i.e. a lie, requires great effort and discipline to maintain. We have to be able to block out contrary evidence, think around internal inconsistencies and cling to a learned framework of thoughts, i.e. a dogma, which is not supported by what we observe around us.

The more an individual's armouring is based on a delusion the more volatile their behaviour is liable to be. There are more chinks in their armour and so they are going to be angry more of the time.

Where possible we express our anger verbally, but sometimes the anger is too strong and our ability to put it into words insufficient. This is when we resort to violence. As Dr. Bernard LaFayette, Jr. pointed out : "Violence is the language of the inarticulate."

Violence, and to a lesser extent anger itself, invalidates the belief system of the individual who uses it.

There was a case of certain individuals from a particular religious faith who were so offended by a depiction of their central prophet in some cartoons that they killed the cartoonist. In so doing they proclaimed to the world that that faith was incapable of giving them the strength to cope with ridicule. Some have been happy to be martyred for their beliefs because they sensibly recognised that, when execution is the only response one's enemies have left, the moral battle has been won. If one is killed because of one's beliefs alone, that is a strong admission of failure on the part of those who do the killing. On the other hand a faith so weak that it is not sufficient unto itself but requires that others tiptoe around it for fear of hurting it, knows deep down that it is a lie. Violence in the service of religion, from witch burnings to inquisitions to crusades to terrorism, has always been an expression of the fear that comes from weak faith.

Most of the time, the best thing to do is to allow violent individuals to drain as little of our energy as possible. If we can step in directly to get in the way of them hurting someone, that is reasonable, but the way they will change and find health is through the inevitable collapse that will occur if they are left to their own devices.

A New World is Rising

If we have within us an original nature characterised by unconditional love which can be liberated when we feel secure enough to drop our armouring, then what about humanity as a whole?

Dogmas and forms of conformist social behaviour are to humanity what the inflexible character armour is to the individual.

But, just as a sudden breakdown of the armouring can be painful and destructive to the individual, the same applies to social or political structures. Racial conflict in the Balkans was kept repressed for decades by communist oppression. When communism collapsed a bloodbath ensued.

It is much better if repressive structures are gradually eroded by better understanding. But we don't always have much control over what happens in the world. We can try to respond to the emergencies, but supporting oppression because its collapse might unleash violence probably wouldn't be a good idea.

We can, however, see positive things happening in the world as well. The breakdown of old dogmas and conformist behaviours has allowed some of us to be more honest about aspects of our lives, such as sexuality, and has opened up a social space for the exchange of new ideas. If I had lived during the Middle Ages and tried to express some of the ideas I have here, if I was lucky I might have been able to talk to one or two people before I was executed for heresy. Today I might be dismissed as a loony by many, but at least I can reach an audience via the internet.

If dogma and social conformism and oppressive political structures are what is keeping our deeper nature as a species repressed, then, even though the collapse of some parts of that human equivalent to the earth's tectonic plates, may release repressed hostilities that express themselves in violence, the overall direction could be towards health.

Jesus said of the last days : "You will hear of wars and

rumours of wars, but see to it that you are not alarmed. Such things must happen, but the end is still to come. Nation will rise against nation, and kingdom against kingdom. There will be famines and earthquakes in various places. All these are the beginning of birth pains." Matthew 24:6-8.

To me this suggests the very thing I'm describing. The wars are the death throws of the old neurotic world, and the collapse of that world is necessary for the birth of the new.

Religious individuals may assert that Jesus was describing something supernatural which would include his personal return to earthly existence, but I believe that individuals who, for whatever reason, have access to their original nature often speak as that nature using the word "I" to refer to what is perhaps more properly thought of as "us". During psychotic breakdowns individuals very often claim to be Jesus or God. Though they may be confused and what they say may be unreliable, they are merely acknowledging that what we term "God" can speak through any of us when armouring is either non-existent or broken. So the return is the return of the voice not the vessel through which it spoke.

Jesus also said this : "At that time if anyone says to you, 'Look, here is the Christ!' or, 'There he is!' do not believe it. For false Christs and false prophets will appear and perform great signs and miracles to deceive even the elect - if that were possible. See, I have told you ahead of time. 'So if anyone tells you, 'There he is, out in the desert,' do not go out; or, 'Here he is, in the the inner rooms,' do not believe it. For as the lightning comes from the east and flashes to the west, so will be the coming of the Son of Man. Wherever there is a carcass, there the vultures will gather." Matthew 24:23-28

Here we can see that what is being referred to as "the coming of the Son of Man" is not something focused in an individual towards whom others can look for guidance. Rather the phenomenon is something which happens everywhere seemingly in a flash. This is consistent with the concept that the social space opened up by the death of dogmas, repressive regimes and social conformism allows for the decentralised improvisation of a new consciousness by those whose thinking has been thus liberated. I believe this book is a part of that, but only a part. There are many other useful ideas out there. And the internet is a key to this coming together of a new consciousness because it allows for completely decentralised communication similar to that found in the human brain. If we are to be one entity the internet will be our nervous system. The last sentence refers to the dying dogmas. A lot of people, like those vultures, will have their attention focused on those dogmas in their death throws, but the real action is happening elsewhere.

It should be emphasised that there is nothing supernatural about Jesus' predictions. They are descriptions of a generalised pattern of events which would be predictable by anyone with insight into the operation of the system being observed, in this case, human society. Jesus was quite fallible as he predicted that these things would happen within the lives of his own generation.

General Advice on Becoming Free

1. Pleasure is healing. Just as suffering directs our attention towards ourselves, pleasure reassures our deeper nature and allows us to be less armoured. The path towards freedom from needing things is to enjoy them more. Addiction occurs when we need more of something to get the same kick. This formula of decreasing returns may be unavoidable with drugs like heroin. But if we have a strong need for particular kinds of food or material possessions or particular activities, then we need to get over the idea that it is wrong to pamper ourselves and instead of criticising ourselves should really surrender to the pleasure that these things can give us. If we get quality of pleasure we won't be so much of a slave to quantity. Sexual pleasure also is healing. We need to be careful about others' potentially fragile egos and also the possibility of disease, but otherwise sex is something which can heal us and help us to reawaken our ability to bond emotionally with our fellows. And if a partner is not immediately available, masturbation is an easy way to access healing pleasure and thus become more open to the new loving and co-operative society.
2. Scary thoughts can't hurt you if you accept them rather than fighting against them. Also, you are not alone with your disturbing thoughts. These are a common, perhaps near universal, experience. When we express our sick thoughts through sick humour it takes the pressure off of others who have similar thoughts. (The films and books of John Waters, as well as the man himself in interviews and in person, has been a major source of comfort to me.)
3. The truth will set you free. If you can find a way of doing it which feels non-threatening to you, telling truths about yourself which you may have previously hidden can be tremendously liberating. Hopefully some of the ideas in this book can help to provide a context in which being more open and honest about ourselves is not the scary process it once was.

4. Don't criticise anyone if you can help it. Let your behaviour towards them carry the message of a better way of living.

5. Share this book with others and discuss it with them. While we can work on our own healing alone, this is not as powerful as what can come about when we use ideas such as these as a catalyst for more open and spontaneous communication with others.

Keith Johnstone

I highly recommend reading the book *Impro : Improvisation and the Theatre* by Keith Johnstone (Eyre Methuen, 1981). It was the book which helped me more than any other in the formulation of these ideas. Especially the following passage :

"Grotesque and frightening things are released as soon as people begin to work with spontaneity. Even if a class works on improvisation every day for only a week or so, then they start producing very 'sick' scenes : they become cannibals pretending to eat each other, and so on. But when you give the student permission to explore this material he very soon uncovers layers of unsuspected gentleness and tenderness. It is no longer sexual feelings and violence that are deeply repressed in this culture now, whatever it may have been like in *fin-de-siecle* Vienna. We repress our benevolence and tenderness."

Other writers whose ideas helped me greatly were : Wilhelm Reich, Sigmund Freud, Carl Jung, R. D. Laing, Oscar Wilde and William Blake.

A Closing Message

The door to heaven is open to us at any time we are willing to accept that we are of absolutely no importance. The bars of our own hell - the "mind-forged manacles" as Blake put it - are our attempts to justify ourselves or prove our self-worth. Accept that none of this matters and we can see that heaven is all around us. It is there in a child's smile, in the rain that waters the earth, even in the maggots that rise in new life from dead meat. All around us is evidence that life and love are eternal and unbroken by strife and suffering.

Feedback

The author can be contacted at aussiescribbler@dodo.com.au

Also by Joe Blow

Materialism is Masturbation : Essays in Freedom

Two Shaky Towers : A Fable

The Anti-Christ Psychosis

Hurt-Proofing Ourselves

The ebook versions of all of Joe Blow's works are available for free download from Smashwords, I-Tunes, Barnes & Noble and other ebook shops.

Lightning Source UK Ltd.
Milton Keynes UK
UKOW04f1703120615

253426UK00001B/115/P

9 781300 343660